SHATTERED DREAMS:
The Story Of
Mary Todd Lincoln

Notable Americans

SHATTERED DREAMS:
The Story of
Mary Todd Lincoln

David R. Collins

MORGAN
REYNOLDS
Incorporated

Greensboro

SHATTERED DREAMS:
The Story of Mary Todd Lincoln

Copyright © 1994 by David R. Collins

Cover photo and frontispiece courtesy of the Library of Congress

Library of Congress Cataloging-in-Publication Data
Collins, David R.
Shattered dreams : the story of Mary Todd Lincoln / David R. Collins. — 1st ed.
    p. cm. -- (Notable Americans)
  Includes bibliographical references and index.
  ISBN 1-883846-07-2 (cloth)
  1. Lincoln, Mary Todd, 1818-1882- --Juvenile literature.
2. Presidents' spouses--United States--Biography--Juvenile literature. 3. Lincoln, Abraham,
1809-1865--Juvenile literature.
[1. Lincoln, Mary Todd, 1818-1882 . 2. First ladies. 3. Women—Biography]   I. Title.
II. Series.
E457 . 25 . L55C65 1994
973.7' 092 -- dc20
[B]
                                                                              93-44792
                                                                                  CIP
                                                                                   AC

Printed in the United States of America

5 4 3 2 1   First Edition

476475

CONTENTS

TRIAL IN CHICAGO

May 19, 1875.

Finally, the day had come. Mary Todd Lincoln rose early that morning, wanting plenty of time to prepare herself for the day ahead. So often in the past she had spent hours selecting just the right gown or just the proper hat. Anything to emphasize her rich brunette hair or the rosy cheeks for which she had so often received compliments. Gloves. Of course, she had to wear gloves. She thought that gloves helped to hide those ugly hands that emphasized her short, plump frame.

But on this particular May morning, Mary Todd Lincoln had no desire to appear stylish. She dressed modestly in a violet muslin dress, accented by a lace collar and a cameo brooch at the neck. No one would label this outfit frivolous, not even her most severe critics.

The light, steady rain falling on the Cook County Courthouse in Chicago cast an eerie greyness to the setting. It appeared more like dusk than morning. In the hallway Mary ignored the arm of the attendant who walked beside her. She wanted no assistance. With sure, determined steps the proud woman strode forward. What lay ahead would be painful, there was no doubt of that. But in the past years Mary Todd Lincoln had known suffering often. She had buried her parents, her husband, and three of her children. Now, Robert, her sole surviving son, was putting her through an agony different than any she had suffered before. During the next hours a court would determine whether or not she was legally insane.

Moments later the attendant directed Mary Lincoln to a courtroom, where she was seated at a table. Asked if she were comfortable, Mary simply nodded. Comfortable? Could she be comfortable listening to people who claimed she was insane? Can she be comfortable knowing that her own flesh and blood thought she could not take care of herself?

In the hours that followed, Mary quietly listened to witnesses called before the court. One by one they testified, doctors and friends, each sharing their observations.

One physician spoke about her terrible headaches, those throbbing, pounding hours of misery. Once she had described her headache as feeling like an Indian was removing the bones of her face and pulling wires out of her eyes. The doctor termed her description "an hallucination," and some people in the courtroom lifted their eyebrows. After all, no one in a proper state of mind would use such a description, would they?

And then there was the unusual incident about a fellow taking her pocketbook. Although it had happened in Chicago, Mary Lincoln was convinced she had seen the same man in Florida. She termed the man "a Wandering Jew." After all, the thief was wearing a long dark coat, sideburns and a beard. So many Jews dressed that way. It was not a slap at the Jewish faith, just a simple description. But maybe others listening thought it cruel and unfair.

Then there were her feelings of persecution—that constant fear that she was being followed, that she was always in danger. Witnesses testified to those times after sundown when she kept the gas lights burning "to scare away the night." When food tasted a bit strange, she was convinced it was poisoned. Often she feared dining out in public, frightened that someone would "do her in."

In an endless parade, the witnesses came. Mary listened to every word in the courthouse, her outer appearance attempting to hide the pain within. The rosy pink had long ago faded from her cheeks.

Finally, Robert rose to testify. The eyes of mother and son met, sharing the tragedy of this moment, the anguish of what was happening. But he had come to the court to do what he believed was necessary. No longer could he trust his mother to take care of her own affairs, to handle money and to look after herself. She had always been kind to him, he told the courtroom, and it was only his love and duty as her son which brought him to "this necessary moment."

As Robert spoke, he wept. He recalled how often Mary imagined things and acted on impulse. The previous March while she was living in Florida, she had telegraphed Robert's physician in Chicago. "My belief is my son is ill; telegraph. I start for Chicago tomorrow." Then she had telegraphed Robert himself. "My dearly beloved son, Robert T. Lincoln — Rouse yourself and live for your mother; you are all I have; from this hour all I have is yours, I pray every night that you may be spared to your mother."

Immediately Robert sent word that he was in fine health and that his mother should stay in Florida. But it was too late. She was already on her way. When she arrived in Chicago, and found him well, she refused to stay at Robert's home. Concerned for her welfare, he took a room adjoining his mother's at the Grand Pacific Hotel. She could not, or would not, sleep. Once she left her room only partially dressed. With a hotel employee's help, Robert led her back to her room. "You are going to murder me!" Mary Lincoln wailed.

In addition to Mary's mental state, there was much concern about her finances. She carried great amounts of money and valuable securities with her—forty and fifty thousand dollars on some occasions. She often went on wild spending sprees, buying clothes she would never wear. It was, of course, no secret that Mary Todd Lincoln enjoyed the very best of fashion. During her years in the White House, her shopping sprees and lavish wardrobe had been a constant topic of gossip. "The President probably wears the first suit he ever owned," some would whisper. "But that woman of his probably never wears the same dress twice." Cruel, vicious remarks. "Stabs," the President had called them. Mrs. Abraham Lincoln had done little to attract admirers as the nation's First Lady.

Yet now, as Robert Lincoln shared the tales of his mother's careless handling of money, there were those who thought differently about Mary Todd Lincoln. Maybe, just maybe, it was an illness that caused her to throw money away without thinking. Perhaps she could not control herself. But if her reckless spending continued, she would use up all that she owned. The thought caused more than one spectator's head to shake sadly in the courtroom. Surely no one wished the widow of the country's great and martyred president to be without financial means. That fear, as well as a loving concern for her well-being, had brought Robert to this hearing. For him to help her, she had to be declared legally insane.

Through the endless hours of testimony that day, Mary Todd Lincoln sat in silence. There was no opportunity for her to speak in her own defense. She could only watch, listen, and wait.

Then it was over. The jury did not take long to reach a decision. Mary Todd Lincoln was ruled "legally insane." Her name was added to the "Lunatic Record" of the Cook County Court, and she was ordered "committed to a State hospital for the Insane."

The verdict read, Robert came to her and took her hand.

His drawn, tired face still revealed the trails of tears which had streamed down his cheeks. "It's for the best, Mother," he whispered.

Mary Lincoln gazed evenly at her son. "Oh, Robert, to think that my son would ever have done this." Her voice did not tremble or falter; her face showed no emotion.

Later that night of May 19, 1875, Mary Todd Lincoln sat quietly in a Chicago hotel room, with guards posted just outside her door. The next morning she would be taken to a private sanitarium in Batavia, Illinois. It seemed a tragic fate for a woman who had started life in a happy home in Lexington, Kentucky, so many years before.

RULES, RULES, RULES!

The stately home of Robert Smith Todd on Short Street in Lexington, Kentucky, was well known to the city residents. Fan-shaped windows above the front door gleamed in the sunlight. While most gentlemen of the city practiced only one occupation, the six-foot, handsome Master Todd was a banker, a merchant, a manufacturer, and a farmer. And he was successful at each!

Mrs. Todd, that is, Eliza Ann Parker Todd, thrived in her position as mistress of the house. Although she took her role as mother and homemaker seriously, like other wealthy Kentuckians of the time Eliza Todd relied heavily on slaves to help run the home. Coachmen, butlers, cooks, maids— all were typically found among the wealthier folks in Lexington.

Mary Ann Todd was born in the family home on December 13, 1818. One of the Negro servants was immediately appointed to look after the new child's needs.

Mammy Sally, the domestic chosen to look after Mary, loved children and welcomed the opportunity to care for the latest addition to the Todd family. It was not long before the girl climbed into the big woman's lap to hear stories, or just to share the events of the day. Often Mary played games with her older sisters Elizabeth and Frances, whom everyone but Master and Mrs. Todd called "Lizzie" and "Fanny." Later there was little Ann, a younger sister whom Mary enjoyed mothering herself. For an extra bit of spice, there were her brothers, Levi and George Todd, guaranteed to liven up any family picnic or party.

As lively as the Todd children were, whenever their actions became too unruly, they were reminded of their noteworthy ancestors and the fine family heritage they were obligated to maintain. Mary's great-grandfather was General Andrew Porter, a leader in the American Revolution. A great-uncle, John Todd, was a companion of the famed explorer George Rogers Clark. Her grandfather, Levi Todd, was a major general of the militia and friend to the noted politician Henry Clay.

The family into which Mary was born was emminent, a mixture of Parkers and Todds related as cousins or in-laws by marriage or descent. The two grandfathers, Levi Todd and Robert Parker, had been founding fathers of the community in the years directly after the Revolutionary War. Under their leadership, Lexington had changed from a few cabins in the shadow of a small wilderness fort to be, along with the much larger New Orleans, the only outposts of genteel sophistication in the unsettled country west of the Allegheny mountains. To be a Todd or a Parker was to be an achiever, and although the times severely restricted a woman's pursuits, Mary Ann Todd was expected to distinguish herself.

In 1824, Mary headed off to school, which took the form of a two story building on the corner of Second and Market Streets. Dr. John Ward ran the academy as both schoolmaster and minister. Tall and slender, he supervised the education of some one hundred and twenty of Lexington's finest offspring. As a teacher, he relied on heavy doses of memorization, recitation and composition. He leaned toward the classics for education—an intense study of Latin, the correct use of numbers, and an ample supply of "Bible stories to build character."

One afternoon Mary hurried home from school to find one of the servants draping the front door in black crepe. The girl hurried inside, where Mammy Sally awaited, her eyes filled with tears. Mrs. Robert Todd was dead, victim of one of the mysterious fevers of that era which snatched away people with no warning at all.

For a while, Robert Todd's sister came to live in the Lexington family home. The six children also spent many hours next door at their Grandmother Parker's. But after an appropriate mourning period, Master Todd was encouraged by friends to look for a new wife. In 1826, the search ended when he married a young lady named Betsy Humphreys. Grandmother Parker totally disapproved of the marriage, and she made her six grandchildren promise that they would never forget the "wonderful woman who was their real Ma."

It was an easy promise to keep for Mary Ann Todd. Her new stepmother was fond of saying, "It takes seven generations to make a lady." Clearly, in her opinion, the Todd girls did not qualify. They were too boisterous and free-spirited, too inclined to shout in loud voices and chase their brothers. No, they had been given too loose a rein in their early years. The new Mrs. Todd thought children should speak only when spoken to and show constant respect to their elders. Hands, hair, and face should be kept clean at all times, as well as clothes. Rules, rules, and more rules. Betsy Humphreys Todd made up a new rule each day. But she finally gave up on her stepchildren and began having her own babies, eventually giving birth to nine children of her own. The crowded Todd home on Short Street was seldom quiet, in spite of the mistress's rules.

Mary and the rest of the Todd clan spent as much time outside as they could. When they tired of yard games in the summertime, they headed for a nearby creek where they waded and caught minnows. Wet clothing brought a spanking, but the adventure was worth the price.

During the fall, the Todds explored the nearby woods on the lookout for walnuts. Many nuts were tossed and thrown at each other, yet each child returned home with a filled basket by day's end. The juicy walnuts were tucked safely away for wintertime snacks.

The fireside hearth was the center of fun during the cold months. Hours slipped by quickly with the singing of songs, the telling of stories and jokes. The sounds of popping corn drowned out the happy squeals at times, while fine juicy apples spit and sizzled near the fire.

News that Betsy Humphreys Todd's niece was coming to stay at the home was met with little joy. Already the house bulged with people. How many more could sit at the dinner table? Yet Mary found the new visitor a cheerful addition.

Elizabeth, who was a year older, was quiet and had no trouble obeying her aunt's many rules. Yet she appreciated Mary's lively spirit and sassy tongue. They shared a room and a big canopied bed together, staying up until all hours of the night exchanging whispers and giggles. One day they also shared the brunt of Mrs. Todd's frustration. Envying the hooped skirts the older women wore, Mary and Elizabeth gathered a collection of branches from a favorite weeping willow tree. By candlelight, the two girls carefully sewed the willow branches into muslin dresses, which they planned to wear to Sunday school. After struggling into their outfits one Sunday morning, they tiptoed down the staircase toward the front door. They got only as far as the front hallway. There stood Mrs. Todd, herself attired in a perfectly hooped skirt. The woman put her hands on her hips and laughed. Mary and Elizabeth exchanged glances. How silly they looked, the branches jutting out here and there, the cloth straining to hold its seams.

"Go take those awful things off!" Mrs. Todd ordered. Elizabeth retreated instantly, not looking up. But Mary bit her lip and glared. Her usual rosy cheeks flared red in anger. Finally, she backed away and ascended the steps. Never had she felt such anger. She never forgave her stepmother for making her feel so foolish.

But if the hooped skirt incident left Mary humiliated, she rejoiced at the debut of a night-blooming cereus. This strange kind of cactus blossomed only at midnight, supposedly only once every hundred years. When the Todds discovered the plant they owned displayed a bud, there was much excitement. A grand party was planned to witness the "coming out" of the cereus. Mary Ann and Elizabeth helped write invitations to friends and neighbors.

The big night arrived. Carriage after carriage arrived bringing satin cloaked gentlemen sporting fancy shirts and puffed ties. Elegant ladies gracefully swished their hoop-skirted dresses into the Todd home, causing Mary and Elizabeth to remember their own efforts trying to put together such stylish attire. As midnight approached, everyone gathered by candlelight to watch the flower. Sure enough, to the amazement and gasps of all nearby, the cereus unfolded its pure white petals on schedule. It was a night to remember—a night like many others that Elizabeth wrote about when she was grown.

If Mary found her stepmother trying at times, she looked with pleasure on those days spent with her step-grandmother Humphreys. The older woman opened her home and her heart to Mary and Elizabeth. The Humphreys home in nearby Frankfort echoed with happy laughter whenever the girls came to visit. There were no warnings about damaging the furniture, or of keeping a spotless face and clean hands. But there were plenty of books, lessons in French and endless conversation.

Grandmother Humphreys was different than anyone Mary had ever met before in many ways. Most wealthy southerners bragged about the number of slaves they owned, and always wanted to own more. Not Grandmother Humphreys. She planned to free her slaves, and wrote so in her will. She talked about President Andrew Jackson and what he was doing in Washington. Back home in Lexington, Mary and Elizabeth were often told that women had no mind for politics. Such topics were to be left to the menfolks. "Nonsense!" scoffed Grandmother Humphreys, and chattered on about the latest tax being discussed in Congress.

Henry Clay, a longtime friend of the Todd family, agreed with Grandmother Humphreys. He had been a famous senator from Kentucky, and Mary was always glad when he visited the Todd house in Lexington. Clay also believed slaves should be set free. By the time she was twelve, Mary

Ann Todd was convinced Henry Clay was the handsomest man in town and had the best manners of anybody, except her own father. She also told Elizabeth, "If I can only be, when I am grown up, just like Grandmother Humphreys, I will be perfectly satisfied with myself."

In 1831, the Todd home buzzed with extra activity. Lizzie, Mary's oldest sister, was going to marry Ninian Edwards of Illinois. The groom's father had been Governor of that state, and nothing would do but that the Todds put on an elegant Southern wedding. The event proved to be the social event of the season, with people exclaiming they had never witnessed such a grand affair. As for Mary, she loved every moment until the time came for Lizzie to head west with her new husband. Never having gone beyond a day's carriage ride distance herself, the thought of journeying so far away was unbelievable! Illinois seemed like the other side of the world.

Later that year, Mary Ann Todd completed her training at Dr. Ward's Academy. Young men whose families enjoyed money and position continued their formal education during these times, but few felt the need for women to continue. It was more important, or so people thought, that they be schooled in the social arts of becoming "ladies of society."

Almost fourteen, Mary was now pushed in the same direction.

For Mary's education in the "social graces," a boarding school run by Madame Victorie Mentelle was selected. Classes were held five days a week in a sprawling, ivy-covered house near Ashland, Henry Clay's home. The Todd family coachman picked Mary up on Monday morning and returned her safely each Friday night. Because Elizabeth was not considered a true Todd, she was left at home. This separation was a source of bitterness for Mary, another wedge between her and her stepmother.

Training at Madame Mentell's school centered around learning all the social graces required for mingling with the best of society. The young ladies mastered different forms of dancing, and the art of pleasant conversation. Knowing how to arrange flowers was important too, as well as the practical rules of managing servants in a household. The proper etiquette in writing letters and invitations received attention, and responding to notes and courtesy requests.

Grandmother Humphreys had provided an appetizer in French; now Madame Mentelle offered an entire meal. The girls in the school learned to speak as fluently as young Parisians. They even put on a French play, with Mary in the lead role.

Mary Ann Todd waltzed her way smoothly through the four years she spent at Madame Mentelle's school. During that time, her older sister Fanny headed west, to join their sister Lizzie in Illinois. But still the family grew. The Todds moved into a bigger house on Main Street. Each year a new baby arrived to fill any vacancy created by a family member moving out.

The life of a young woman in Lexington of that era was much different than it would be today. Women lived in the shadow of their husbands. Their main purpose in life was considered to be a wife and mother, and an efficient manager of the household. Cooking, cleaning, laundry, and the care and instruction of children were the paramount duties.

In well-to-do families, girls were instructed in how to supervise slaves or domestic workers, who actually performed the chores. In an age before television and movie theatres, the main forms of entertainment were visits by family, friends, and neighbors. A neat, orderly house, and well-prepared food and drink for guests, was considered the duty of a good wife.

In this atmosphere, only about one out of a hundred women failed to marry. The fear of being a "spinster" or "old maid" was real and urgent. An unmarried woman had almost no opportunity to make a living on her own, and was dependent on the charity of male relations for her survival. Little thought was given to a girl's academic education because practical skills would make her a more attractive mate. Even girls from privileged families had only a year or two of instruction in reading or writing and mathematics. Social skills were far more important: the art of polite parlor conversation; sewing, knitting, and crocheting; and perhaps instruction in music or French to add a touch of refinement and sophistication.

In 1837, Mary traveled west to visit her sisters. Although Springfield, Illinois, lacked the culture and refinement of life in Lexington, it was different and exciting, a taste of pioneer life Mary had never experienced. The town had recently become the state capitol of Illinois. She liked the city, especially when she found out there were two men for every woman. The parties and fancy balls she attended upon her return to Lexington could not replace the special feeling of adventure she had in Springfield. She sought out Dr. Ward, her old teacher, borrowed books from his library and memorized romantic poems by the hour. But her reading only made her more restless. Her life as a Southern belle in Lexington now seemed tiresome and empty.

It was not long before an opportunity to escape presented itself. Mary's sisters offered to let her come and live with them in Springfield. Mary accepted the invitation eagerly.

In October of 1839, Mary Ann Todd bid farewell to her Lexington family. To her father, her brothers and sisters, it was a sad good-bye. To her stepmother, it was a welcome departure. The woman had created, in Mary's words, a "desolate" atmosphere in the Todd home, and Mary was eager to escape. The future was uncertain, but the plump 5'3" brunette who boarded the train in the Lexington depot was eager to begin a new life in Springfield, Illinois.

ENTER ABRAHAM LINCOLN

The arrival of Mary Ann Todd hardly went unnoticed among the residents of Springfield, particularly the young bachelors. She had barely rested from her trip—it took a week by train, riverboat and stagecoach—before she was starting to receive gentleman callers. Fanny had married a Springfield physician, William Wallace, and they welcomed the opportunity to introduce the new arrival.

How quiet the Edwards house seemed compared to the house back in Lexington. It sat on a hillside away from the center of town, and there were no clusters of children squealing and hollering at all hours. There were no Negro slaves around either, because Illinois was a free state. Families of social standing in Springfield often employed house servants for cooking and cleaning.

The Edwards parlor was a gathering place for Springfield's young social set. Mary was a vital member among this group, which called itself "The Coterie." They shared book reviews and offered poetry readings among themselves. Mary's reading with Dr. Ward, and her knowledge of French from Madame Mentelle, impressed the group. They also were amazed at the young woman's flair for style in clothing. She seemed never to wear the same outfit twice. The best shops in Springfield had orders to let Mary Ann Todd know whenever a new shipment of dresses arrived from the East. Nothing would prevent this fancy young Lexington belle from wearing the very best and latest styles.

Shopping was sometimes difficult. Often the roads and paths leading downtown were filled with water and mud. There were no paved streets or sidewalks. It did not bother the men much because they wore high, heavy boots. But fashionable women wore no such protection. Nor was it "ladylike" to lift one's dress—the ankle might show. Yet when Mary felt like going shopping, nothing could stop her. One morning she persuaded a favorite friend, Mercy Levering, to join her on a jaunt downtown. In their arms, Mary and Mercy carried a bundle of shingles. Carefully they laid a shingle at a time ahead of them, step by step, as they walked. Some folk shook their heads in disbelief, while others openly laughed and applauded the women's re-

Mary Todd Lincoln in Springfield, 1846. (Library of Congress)

sourcefulness. Whatever the case, Mary gained attention—and she *did* enjoy being noticed.

It was the same way at parties. Despite her plump short frame, Mary swirled around the dance floor with poise and grace. Often she learned what other ladies were going to wear, and then she added an extra flower or two. She always seemed to have plenty to say during conversations, making even the most awkward gentleman feel at ease. On December 16, 1839, she had the opportunity to test those skills.

The place was The American House, Springfield's finest hotel. The occasion was the Cotillion Party, welcoming in the forthcoming holidays. It was the social event of the year, anticipated by anyone of position in Springfield. Mary Ann Todd purchased a special ball gown for the evening, much to her sister's displeasure. Elizabeth had tired of her sister's extravagances, and her constant desire to attract attention. But when Mary made up her mind about something, she could not be restrained.

The candles glowed brightly in the ballroom; handsomely costumed attendants stood at each doorway. Mary and Mercy floated in together, eager to be noticed by any and all eligible young men present. Since the state legislature was in session, many of the fellows were from out of town.

"Hello, Molly!" someone called out. Mary turned, knowing the greeting had come from a member of the Coterie group. Several of her friends called her "Molly."

Mary called back a greeting. She always sparkled at a social gathering, eager to share the latest gossip about fashion, people and events. Sometimes her sisters urged her not to be so talkative, and certainly not to talk about politics! But Grandmother Humphreys had left her imprint. Mary Ann Todd would talk about anything she wished. There was no such thing as "men talk" and "women talk." There was just talk.

One by one, gentlemen appeared before Mary, introducing themselves and requesting a dance. She obliged with a grateful smile. Surely, the years with Madame Mentelle had equipped her well. There was a Howard Swanson, a Franklin Harrington, and Abraham Lincoln.

Now that was a familiar name. Mary knew she recognized it, yet the tall, thin fellow standing before her was a total stranger. She searched her memory as she studied the man in the long-tailed black coat and satin vest, with a white shirt set off by a muffler-like tie called a "stock" which swirled into a small bow. Almost 31, he looked older with his grey eyes, leathery skin, and dark unruly hair resting atop a long slender face. Suddenly Mary smiled. She remembered now who this fellow was. He was the junior law partner of her cousin, John Todd Stuart.

"Miss Todd, I want to dance with you in the worst way," Lincoln offered. His voice shook a bit; he was clearly nervous. Mary took his jitters as a compliment.

But once the couple was on the dance floor, Lincoln's clumsiness proved he had not misled his partner. Many years later, Mary would tell the story. "Mister Lincoln asked to dance with me in the worst way," she said, "and he did exactly that."

But if Mary Todd was not impressed with Abraham Lincoln's dancing, she was delighted with his conversation. There was a gentleness about the man, whether he spoke of people or politics, a topic of intense interest to both. Not only was he a law associate of her cousin, he was also a state legislator serving with her brother-in-law, Ninian Edwards. Towering above her, Lincoln listened closely to her every word, often chuckling and adding a witty comment. When Mister Lincoln asked if he might call upon her, Mary quickly—but not too quickly—gave her consent.

Although Abraham Lincoln is now considered to be one of the greatest Americans, and generally considered to be the best President to ever have served, he seemed a curious mixture of a man to the people who knew him. He was a different type of man, and perhaps it was this difference that first attracted Mary Todd.

Lincoln's mother died when he was a young boy, and his father, Thomas Lincoln, was a hard-working, but illiterate farmer. There was never much closeness between father and son. When Lincoln left home at age 21, he never visited his father again, and did not attend his funeral.

Lincoln grew into a moody and introspective young man, often described as "melancholy." Yet he had a wonderful sense of humor and was an excellent teller of stories and jokes. From a very early age he developed a love for reading and ideas, and as an adult mastered a clear but eloquent writing style. It is said that as an adolescent he would place a borrowed book between the handles of a plow and would read it while resting the mule or horse at the end of a furrow.

After leaving home, Lincoln educated himself, passed the bar exam, and began practicing law. An ambitious man, he was somewhat ashamed of his frontier beginnings and wanted to enter "genteel" society. Tall and clumsy, with a homely face and long, thin neck, he sought the approval of friends and townspeople. He needed the respect of his peers.

This may be the reason he was so ambitious, especially for public office. "I have no other ambition so great as that of being truly esteemed of my fellow man, by rendering myself worthy of their esteem," he once declared.

As the new year arrived, Abraham Lincoln became a regular caller at the Edwards home. He, however, was certainly not the only gentleman interested in Miss Mary Ann Todd.

One other contender was Stephan A. Douglas. Short and stocky, he was a leading Democrat in Illinois politics. Mary was fascinated by his agile mind, and the two spent hours discussing great books they had read.

Edwin Webb was another suitor who appeared often at the Edwards door. Eighteen years older than Mary, he was a widower with two children. It was clear to everyone that he was looking for a wife.

As for Mary Ann Todd, she was just looking. It was pleasing indeed to welcome so many gentlemen callers. Elizabeth Edwards offered her opinions freely and often, one being that she did not consider Abraham Lincoln suitable. Oh, he might be a good lawyer and decent in character, but he hardly possessed the social graces necessary for a potential husband.

Mary hardly needed reminding of Mister Lincoln's shortcomings. But for every weakness, there was a strength about the man. So what if he pronounced some words like a backwoodsman? It was *what* he said that was important, not how he spoke. Unlike so many men of the times, he appreciated a woman's view about politics. He might not have read many books, but the ones he had read, he read thoroughly. And he admired and respected the old Todd family friend, Henry Clay. Mary could not talk enough about the former senator.

In June of 1840, Mary traveled to Columbia, Missouri, to visit relatives. Who should show up in that strange town but Mister Abraham Lincoln! It was a welcome surprise, one that showed Mary she had a serious suitor on her hands. Yet this was no time for commitment. Before long, she was writing Mercy Levering about another, unnamed fellow she had met in Missouri. He was "an agreeable lawyer & grandson of Patrick Henry—what an honor!" Despite the gentleman's proposal, Mary wrote, in the dramatic language she used throughout her life, "Uncle and others think, he surpasses his noble ancestor in talents, yet Merce I love him not, & my hand will never be given, where my heart is not."

Upon her return to Springfield, Mary found Lincoln eagerly waiting. More and more often he appeared in the parlor of Ninian Edwards. Before long, when the weather permitted, they strolled along the city's pathways, sharing quiet conversation. In December of 1840, the holiday chatter included the engagement of Miss Mary Ann Todd and Mister Abraham Lincoln.

"LOVE IS ETERNAL"

Not everyone in Springfield was thrilled with the engagement announcement of Mary Ann Todd and Abraham Lincoln. Certainly Stephan Douglas and Edwin Webb were disappointed. But Ninian Edwards and his wife were devastated. Elizabeth shared her objections openly. What kind of choice was this for a lady with a Todd pedigree? Besides, the man was almost ten years older than Mary! (That Edwin Webb was eighteen years older was suddenly forgotten.)

Furthermore, Lincoln had no formal schooling. The little education he did have was self-acquired. He offered no impressive family background, only a sprinkling of relatives that reflected no money or social position. He owned no home or property. He could hardly be considered handsome, with always a tuft of hair out of place or a suit that seemed to hang rather than rest on his long-boned frame. Ninian Edwards merely shook his head at his sister-in-law's choice, but Lizzie continued to criticize Mary's husband-to-be.

Mary held her ground. She declared she didn't merely want a man with "gold." Other factors were more important. "I would rather marry a good man—a man of mind—with a hope and bright prospects ahead for & position—fame and power," she stated.

But the lack of "gold" *did* trouble Abraham Lincoln. It was not merely that he was poor. He was in debt. He could not offer Mary a grand home or even a humble house. He lived in a boardinghouse, and they probably would have to start out that way too. Could she tolerate such an existence? There certainly would be few funds for her clothing. How would Mary accept that?

Abraham buried himself in his work, hoping to save a little extra money for the future. The oil lamp burned long into the night at Lincoln's law desk. He took extra legal cases, traveling by horse or carriage, riding over the dusty roads into smaller Illinois towns and villages. It was a common practice for lawyers of the day to "ride the judicial circuit," taking cases in whatever town or village they visited.

In the fall of 1841, the couple was scheduled to attend a

dance together. As usual, Mary dressed in plenty of time and waited for Lincoln to appear at the Edwards home. When he did not arrive on time, Mary grew annoyed. It was not the first time he had been late. Annoyance quickly led to anger. Off she went to the dance without him. Soon after her arrival, she spotted Stephan Douglas in the crowd and rushed to his side. Caught up in his work, Lincoln had not noticed the late hour. When he did, he hurried to the Edwards home where he was told Mary had gone on without him. Arriving at the dance, he saw Mary laughing and enjoying herself on the arm of Mister Douglas. Lincoln sadly left the dance without saying a word to Mary.

Surely Mary expected her "Mister Lincoln" to come begging forgiveness. But when he did not, she became frustrated. Maybe her sister was right. Perhaps Stephan Douglas would be a better choice. Or Edwin Webb.

Finally, on New Year's Day of 1841, Abraham Lincoln appeared at the Edwards doorstep. He looked tired, far older than his years. He told Mary that he was sorry he had hurt her and that he probably could never give her the kind of life she deserved. He asked for her to release him from the engagement.

Certainly, Mary would not want a man who did not want

her. The engagement was broken. Lincoln left the house feeling even more miserable than when he had entered. He went into a deep depression, and did not leave his room for a week.

The break-off of the engagement was devastating to Lincoln. Earlier, he had broken off an engagement to another woman, Mary Owen, on the grounds he was too poor for her. He broke that engagement off with a series of emotional letters that revealed his deep insecurity regarding women and romance. It was probably the resistance of Elizabeth and Ninian Edwards to him as a suitor that brought back the feelings of worthlessness that caused him to end the engagement with Mary.

His deep misery was obvious when, on January 23, a little over three weeks after that "fateful first," he wrote to John Todd Stuart, his law partner and Mary's cousin. "I am now the most miserable man living," wrote Lincoln. "If what I feel were equally distributed to the whole human family, there would not be one cheerful face on the earth." Lincoln promised he would avoid all parties and dances where Mary might be. Perhaps not seeing her would help ease the pain.

Ninian and Elizabeth Edwards, however, were delighted

The earliest known photo of Abraham Lincoln, taken in 1846. (Library of Congress)

with the news of the broken engagement. They thought Mary had come to her senses before making a horrible mistake. Word circulated around Springfield that the young lady from Lexington was again receiving callers. Edwin Webb took the news cheerfully, and his visits began all over again. Mary entertained him with a smile and good humor, but confided in Mercy that her "heart could never be his."

Much of Lincoln's time was spent away from Springfield, fighting legal battles across the Illinois countryside. Keeping his promise, he stayed away from social gatherings where Mary might be present. Despite these efforts, his feelings for Mary seemed to have changed little. By the spring of 1842, there was still no news that she was engaged to anyone else. Lincoln felt that he might be responsible for her unhappiness and wrote that such an awareness "still kills my soul."

One of Lincoln's good friends in the state legislature, Joshua Speed, was also struggling with romantic problems. By coincidence, his romantic interest was also a young woman who lived in Kentucky. She was still there, and the romance was based largely on letters. Speed had been quite a favorite of young ladies of the time, and the thought of "settling down" with just one woman scared him. Speed frequently sought out Lincoln's advice.

Early in 1842, Joshua Speed and his love Fanny Henning were wed. Lincoln's writings reflect a personal pride in the part he played in bringing his colleague and his sweetheart together. No doubt he wondered why he could not be so successful in his own situation. He was unable to put Mary Todd out of his thoughts.

Two mutual friends managed to pull Mary and Abraham together again. For sixteen months their paths had not crossed. Then, Mr. and Mrs. Simeon Francis arranged for the two former lovers to meet at the Francis home—without telling them. Surely Mary Todd and Abraham Lincoln were surprised to see each other. Every indication is that they immediately pushed aside the past, patched up their differences, and went on from there.

Future meetings were held in private. Ninian and Elizabeth Edwards were still deadset against any reconciliation, and Lincoln could not go calling on Mary as long as she lived under the Edwards roof. He did not like being sneaky about the matter, but it had to be done. The Francis home proved a frequent meeting spot. Friends were used to pass messages, spoken or written, between Mary Todd and Abraham Lincoln. Once again, marriage plans became a topic of conversation between the two. Lincoln visited a jeweler and ordered an inscription for a wedding band. The engraving read "Love Is Eternal."

November 4, 1842, was the day picked for the wedding. Mary waited until the last moment before telling her sister and brother-in-law. They were both shocked. Elizabeth ranted and raved, and Mary raved and ranted right back. The wedding would be held that very night at the minister's home. If Ninian and Elizabeth wished to come, they were welcome. If not, so be it. Mary was not going to listen to another word.

The Edwards saw there was nothing more they could say. But to have a wedding at the minister's house? That would certainly not do—not for a Todd of Lexington, Kentucky. Quickly Ninian and Elizabeth made plans to host the wedding in their own home. Sister Frances was sent for, coachmen were dispatched to invite Springfield's "finest," and the Edwards kitchen became the center for preparing a wedding cake and punch.

By evening, winds tossed a heavy mist across Springfield. Carriages carrying thirty of the city's socially elite rolled up in front of the Edwards home. Servants dressed in their finest uniforms welcomed the guests, and saw to their high hats, cloaks and capes. Then they were led into the living room. At the appropriate time, the Episcopal minister, Dr. Charles Dresser, appeared before the fireplace and opened a small black Bible. The couple faced the mantel, allowing the guests to behold a remarkable contrast—Lincoln standing 6'4" and wearing a black suit, gazing down at Mary, only 5'3", in a white dress.

"I, Mary, take thee Abraham..."

It was a short service, simple but dignified. Well-wishers surrounded the newly married couple after it was over, and then it was off to the dining room to sample the wedding cake hastily prepared that afternoon.

Later, Mr. and Mrs. Abraham Lincoln slipped into a carriage and headed to a modest boardinghouse where they would spend their first night as husband and wife. No doubt Mary touched her wedding band many times during those hours of November 4, 1842. "Love Is Eternal." It was a perfect inscription...

LIFE IN SPRINGFIELD

The Globe Tavern was a plain two story structure topped off by a bell on the roof. The ringing of the bell signaled the arrival of a stagecoach, sending stablemen running to take care of the horses. The accommodations were hardly what Mary Ann Todd was used to, but, she was no longer Mary Ann Todd. As Mary Lincoln, her life would change. The couple's sparse new living space at the Globe was a hint to those changes. The cost for room and board was only eight dollars a week, and for the present, it would do.

On February 12, 1843, Abraham Lincoln observed his 34th birthday at the Globe. The party was small, yet that did not lessen the happy mood. Mary Lincoln declared "I am so glad you have a birthday. I feel so grateful to your mother."

For Mary had learned she was pregnant. The parents-to-be looked forward to the arrival of their first child, but it added pressure on the new marriage. Pregnant women and nursing mothers kept their "delicate" condition as private as possible, and seldom showed themselves in public. Mary would be somewhat isolated at the Globe. Abraham desperately wanted to find a more suitable home to raise a family, which meant he had to work even longer hours to earn more money. But, more than ever, both he and Mary hated the time he had to spend "traveling the circuit" as a lawyer. A colleague noted that Lincoln was "desperately homesick" while away from Springfield and could hardly wait to get back.

When Lincoln was home he was not always easy to live with. Although kind and considerate, Mary often found traits to criticize in her new husband. His table manners, or lack of them, were a continual trial for someone who had grown up in a genteel household. He had no sense of style or color in his clothes; his career might have suffered had Mary not continually monitored which suits, shirts, and trousers were purchased and which were worn together.

Always a light eater, Abraham was continually late for meals. Absentminded, he often forgot social appointments. Mary often had to send someone to fetch Mr. Lincoln home.

He had a habit of stretching out on the hallway floor for a nap, and enjoyed reading newspaper articles out loud. He sometimes answered the front door in his undershirt, which in that day was a serious breach of decorum.

But, by far the greatest burden for Mary throughout their marriage was her husband's frequent and prolonged absence from home. The life of a frontier lawyer involved "riding the circuit," following the judge from town to town to earn his living arguing criminal and civil cases. From 1846, the year his second son was born, until 1860 when he was elected president, Lincoln was away from home nearly half the time. In 1850, for example, he was on the road away from Springfield for 190 days.

On August 1, 1843, Mary Todd Lincoln gave birth to a baby son. With love and tenderness, the father hovered over his wife, hoping that his presence might comfort her. From that day on, Mary referred to her husband as "Father." Lincoln, himself, who had usually called his wife "Molly" in the past, now began to refer to her as "Mother."

Lincoln had initially planned to call the baby Joshua out of affection for his friend Joshua Speed, but Mary was firm in her choice of Robert Todd, in honor of her own father, and she would not be swayed. Not wanting to cause problems, Joshua Speed was silent on the matter, flattered that Lincoln had even considered his name.

As soon as arrangements could be made, Mary's father traveled from Lexington to greet his new grandson. "May God bless and protect my little namesake," Robert Todd whispered to the child. The man informed his son-in-law that he could count on a yearly contribution of $125 until Lincoln was more firmly established in his law practice. That was a considerable amount of money in those days, and Lincoln was humbled and grateful for the gift. Not only that, Mister Todd also helped clear up the tension that had existed between Mary and her two sisters since the wedding. From what he had seen of Abraham Lincoln, he appeared to be a loving husband, a caring father and a gentleman, and he saw no reason why his daughters should not approve of the marriage. His effort toward family peace having been largely successful, Robet Todd returned to Lexington in high spirits.

Mary and Abraham Lincoln had grown used to the clanging bell atop the Globe Tavern. They ignored the sounds of the other boarders and guests. Little "Bobbie," as they called their new son, could do neither. The noise of the bell and of other tenants woke up the infant. He, in turn, then woke up the neighbors with his high-pitched squeals. Clearly, a new home was needed.

A three-room frame house at 214 South Fourth Street offered temporary living space, although the new parents had no desire to occupy the cramped quarters for long. They moved in during September of 1843.

By the end of the year, Lincoln heard rumors that Dr. Dresser's home on the corner of Eighth and Jackson might be for sale. The story-and-a-half house was not far from Lincoln's law office. Not only that, there was a fenced back yard just beckoning any young child to play.

Rumor became fact. In January of 1844, Lincoln drew up a contract to buy Dr. Dresser's home for $1200 plus a lot on Adams Street valued at $300. It was May before the family gained possession, but Mary and Abraham Lincoln wore happy smiles. This was, after all, their first real home.

Quickly, Mary learned that running a household was no easy task, especially when one member was an infant. Bobbie often picked the worst times to cry. Sometimes it was when Mary ducked outside to get a bucket of water from the backyard pump. Sometimes it was when she had a full meal cooking on the iron stove in the kitchen. Or sometimes it was when she was baking a loaf of bread or

Robert Todd Lincoln as a student at Harvard. (National Archives)

a pan of breakfast biscuits. None of these chores came easily to Mary, but to save money she rarely used the hired farm girls other Springfield wives turned to for help. Whenever family guests came from Lexington, Mary invited them to prepare their favorites dishes in the kitchen. She watched every move, hoping to improve her own skills. In Lexington, slaves and other servants had always taken care of the cooking and cleaning. Now it was up to Mary. Whenever she was busiest, Bobbie would wail away. Maybe he was hungry or thirsty. Perhaps he'd had "an accident." Or maybe he just wanted attention. In any case, Mary came running. Nothing came before the health and safety of the child.

Despite her workload, Mary enjoyed life in the house on Eighth Street. By the time her husband arrived home from his law office, she was full of stories from her day's activities.

One day's events, however, were anything but cheerful. Like most houses in the neighborhood, the Lincoln dwelling did not have an indoor toilet. Quicklime was kept in the kitchen for the purpose of helping keep the outdoor privy decent-smelling and clean. Once Bobbie was old enough to explore, he managed to find the box containing the lime. He took a mouthful of the poisonous mixture. Seeing what the boy had done, Mary became hysterical. She dashed into the street. "Bobbie will die!" she screamed. "Bobbie will die!" A quick-thinking and quicker-acting neighbor raced out. Learning what had happened, the neighbor ran into the Lincoln house and hastily rinsed the child's mouth out with water. Fortunately, Robert Todd Lincoln showed no ill effects from the event.

But the boy was active and curious, that was certain. Once, while Lincoln sat writing a letter at his law office, he was summoned home by a messenger. Bobbie had run off! Never had the lawyer's long legs moved so fast. By the time he arrived home, the boy had returned. Lincoln returned to his desk and wrote that "by now, very likely he is run away again."

By the fall of 1844, Mary was expecting again. The baby arrived on March 10, 1845, a healthy child with a hearty set of lungs. "It appears there is no such thing as a quiet child named Lincoln," his father observed. The infant was named Edward Baker Lincoln in honor of a close family friend, but the nickname of "Little Eddie" soon gained favor.

There were other ways in which Lincoln's life was changing. His partner and Mary's cousin, John Todd Stuart, had been elected to Congress. After Todd left for Washington, Lincoln entered into a law partnership with a man named Stephen Logan. But Logan soon decided to practice law with his son. William Herndon was Lincoln's third partner. Until this point, Lincoln had always been the junior law partner. Now he became the senior member of the firm. Yet he still agreed to split the profits evenly, an arrangement of which Mary did not approve. In truth, she did not really approve of Mr. Herndon at all. Herndon drank often and heavily, and Mary had little use for that habit. Not only that, he openly expressed his disbelief in God. Mary, raised as a Presbyterian, had attended the Episcopal Church since coming to Springfield. Now, more than once, she raised her voice to complain of William Herndon. Lincoln paid little attention. As long as the man practiced law honestly, it was not his place to judge moral character or habits.

But if they disagreed about William Herndon, Abraham and Mary were totally agreed on Lincoln's future. More than anything else, they both wanted Abraham to have a political career. Mary was certain that her husband could go far in politics. Their dreams reached far beyond the state legislature. When John Todd Stuart decided not to run for the U.S. Congress again, Lincoln toyed with the idea of running himself. But his friend Edward Baker spoke up first. He wanted to be the candidate for the Whigs, a political party with roots all the way back to the Revolution. Lincoln reined in his ambition and was selected as the delegate to nominate Baker at the Whig national convention.

In 1846, Lincoln got his real chance. He had early on expressed his desire to run for Congress. Aware of the young lawyer's increasing popularity, the Whigs agreed. Abraham Lincoln was a candidate for Congress. Mary was ecstatic.

The campaign soon turned ugly. Lincoln's opponent, Peter Cartwright, was a preacher who traveled the country-side. Because Lincoln often seemed reluctant to discuss his personal spiritual beliefs and did not officially belong to a church, Cartwright charged Lincoln with being "anti-Christian" and "without conscience." Mary raged through the house, denouncing "Preacher Peter." She also encouraged her husband to declare himself a "God-fearing Christian." Lincoln shook his head. He did not want his personal religious beliefs to be part of a public campaign. But finally, to please Mary as well as to quiet Cartwright's charges, he issued a statement:

A charge having gone into circulation in some of the neighborhood of this district, in substance that I am an open scoffer of Christianity. That I am not a member of any Christian Church is true; but I have never denied the truth of the Scriptures; and I have never spoken with intentional disrespect of religion in general, or of any denomination of Christians in particular. . . I do not think I could myself, be brought to support a man for office, whom I knew to be an open scoffer at, religion. Leaving the high matter of eternal consequences between him and his Maker, I still do not think any man has the right thus to insult the feelings, and injure the morals, of the community in which he may live. If then, I was guilty of such conduct, I should blame no man who should condemn me for it; but I do blame those, whoever they may be, who falsely put such a charge in circulation against me.

It was not a statement Lincoln enjoyed presenting, yet it was necessary to clear up misunderstandings in the race for Congress. It also seemed necessary to keep peace under his own roof. If Mary Lincoln had been allowed to write the statement, it likely would have been a good deal harsher. Lawyer Abraham Lincoln was well known around Springfield for a gentle manner and thoughtful actions. But Mary was another story. Tales of temper tantrums peppered the gossip among the city's political elite.

Mary became a target of gossip for another reason. For many citizens of Springfield, her enthusiasm for politics was unseemly. It was not considered proper for a wife to involve herself too deeply in her husband's career, especially if that career involved running for office. But Mary had loved the rough and tumble of politics since her girlhood in Kentucky, and had clearly planned to marry a man who shared her interest. In addition, she saw no reason why she should conceal her interest in politics and her husband's career. She let her opinions be known on most issues and decisions. This outspokenness resulted in considerable comments by her more traditional neighbors, and established a pattern of criticism of her political activism that would continue until the day her husband died.

Lincoln's printed answer to Cartwright's criticism worked. Cartwright continued to taunt Lincoln about his spiritual beliefs, but Lincoln had said all he wanted to say on the matter. He argued other issues—taxes, transportation, business promotion—and the people listened.

In November of 1847, the citizens went to vote. Abraham Lincoln tallied 6340 votes to Peter Cartwright's 4829. A celebration party was held at the Lincoln home on the corner of Eighth and Jackson. Mary Lincoln swirled around the room, proudly greeting the guests in the role of victor's wife.

One gentleman present, Ward Hill Lamon from Virginia, had not been in Springfield very long. He remarked that wherever he had stayed in eastern Illinois, people praised Mr. Lincoln. Mary Lincoln laughed. "Yes, he is a great favorite everywhere...He is to be President of the United States some day; if I had not thought so I never would have married him, for you can see he is not very pretty. But look at him. Doesn't he look as if he would make a magnificent President?"

Abraham Lincoln chuckled at the notion, smiling at his ever proud and outspoken wife. Following Lincoln's lead, others nearby laughed politely, and Mary joined them. Yet there was no doubt that she meant exactly what she said.

ON TO WASHINGTON

Packing for a family of four, two of them young children, and moving to the East Coast was no easy chore in 1847. The house at Eighth and Jackson became a collection of boxes, trunks and crates. Mary Lincoln dived into the task with fresh energy, eager to take on the glory and grandeur of a new city—the nation's capital. Of course, it would never do to bypass Lexington on the way. Some of the family had never seen her two darling boys Bobbie and Eddie. Not only that, Abraham Lincoln was now an elected member of the United States House of Representatives! It was a chance to show him off. Whether it be a new satin dress, a plumed feather hat or a husband, Mary Todd Lincoln did enjoy showing off her possessions.

For three weeks the Lincolns visited the Todds. Once again, Mary enjoyed the thrill of being the center of attention. Even her hard-to-please stepmother was impressed. And what a joy to introduce Abraham to her old friend Henry Clay! The two men talked the afternoon away.

In November the Lincoln family headed to the Lexington depot to board a train for Washington, D.C. It had been a triumphant visit among family and friends. Now the challenge of an entire new world lay ahead. Congress was scheduled to convene December 6, 1847, when its newest members would be sworn in.

A boardinghouse near the Capitol offered the best accommodations for the least price. A nearby park featured band concerts every Saturday night, and the Lincolns were grateful for any free entertainment they could find. Despite the advantages, the boardinghouse seemed unable to provide Bobbie and Eddie with enough amusement. Guests complained too, and Mary did not take well to their criticism. She answered them with short, curt remarks, then retired to her room with a headache.

The headaches came more and more often, each one seemingly worse than the one before. No matter how Lincoln tried to comfort his wife, there appeared to be little he could do. Finally, the Lincolns decided it might be best for Mary and her two sons to return to Lexington until his first term was finished.

Back in Kentucky, with slaves and servants to take care of meals and housework, Mary regained her strength and disposition. She missed her husband deeply, however, and her letters reflected this sadness. On his part, he found his rooms "exceedingly tasteless" without her and the boys around. Mary wrote often about their every action. "Do not fear the children have forgotten you," she assured him. Certainly, she had not. "How much," she wrote, "I wish instead of writing, we were together this evening. I feel very sad away from you."

That sadness ended when Lincoln finished his first term in Congress and joined his family for a return to Springfield in October of 1848. The house on Jackson and Eighth had been rented, so the Lincolns stayed once more at the Globe Tavern.

November brought Lincoln back to Washington for another session of the House of Representatives. There was no thought of the rest of the family returning; they remained at the Globe. Christmas was especially difficult for the separated family, yet both "Father" and "Mother" Lincoln eagerly awaited the time when they could be back in their Springfield home together.

That time came early in April of 1848. It was a joyful Mary Todd Lincoln who crossed the doorway of their beloved first home, a hand holding onto each of her sons. Home again!

The joy did not last. News of Robert Todd's death summoned the family back to Lexington in July. Always, her father's face had brightened her childhood and her visits home. Now the house on Main Street seemed empty and sad. Once again, Mary's pounding headaches returned.

Mary was still mourning her father when little Eddie became ill. It was doubly frustrating for her since she had always taken such care to make certain her children stayed healthy. The slightest sneezing or coughing sent her to the cupboard for the Castor Oil or the awful-tasting "Bottle Vermifuge." Just a mention of the latter mixture sent children diving under their beds. Both Mary and her husband hovered around Eddie's bedside, hoping and praying for any sign of improvement. Days became weeks as the boy lay confined to bed. A dispatch arrived bringing word of Grandmother Parker's death in Lexington, but Mary scarcely had time to take in the news. Her own son, not even four years old, was now fighting for his life.

On February 1, 1850, the fight ended. Edward Wallace Lincoln died.

For 52 days Mary and Abraham Lincoln had remained close to their son in his illness. Now he was gone. A tired and haggard father tried to come to terms with this tragedy. But for Mary, there was no understanding, only grief. The tears came, never stopping, and the house was filled with her cries and sobs. Her father, dead only seven months, and now this—it was too much. She did not eat or sleep.

"Eat, Mary, for we must live." Only the constant plea of a comforting husband cut through the curtain of grief. Yes, Eddie, her dear little Eddie was gone, taken away far too early. But there was Abraham to think of, and Bobbie too. Slowly, ever so slowly, Mary Lincoln began to pull herself back to the world of the living.

In the spring of 1850, the Lincolns again headed to Lexington. Mary's family was haggling over her late father's estate, and Abraham Lincoln was considered a calm and honest voice amid the quarreling. At least it was a chance to escape Springfield for a time. But the house at Eighth and Jackson still carried the memories of a lost child when they came back. Often Lincoln would have to apologize for his wife's nervous spells which caused her to be absent from gatherings.

By summertime, Mary Lincoln was pregnant again, a

condition which somewhat lifted her spirits. Both parents-to-be hoped for a girl this time. She looked forward to the closeness she could have with a little girl.

But when the baby arrived on December 21, 1850, it was another boy. No matter. The infant was warmly welcomed as a special Christmas gift. He was promptly christened William Wallace Lincoln, in honor of Mary's brother-in law, Dr. Wallace. As usual, the child soon received a nickname, Willie, which he was called by family and friends.

The new year dawned bright with a new baby in the home. There was little time to look back at the tragedies of the past. Willie demanded constant attention. But he quickly became a favorite of his father. Lincoln delighted in scooping his son up and whirling him around the room. Mary's admonishments of "Take care, Father" went unheard. Before long, the child was pulling the legal papers out of Lincoln's tall black hat. (It was the lawyer's habit to carry documents on his head. Mary scoffed at the practice, but her husband explained it kept the papers safe and out of the rain.) In truth, neither Lincoln attempted to discipline their sons. There were many folks, like law partner Herndon, who considered the boys to be hopelessly spoiled.

By the fall of 1852, Mary was once more expecting a

baby. Surely this time it would be a girl! Both parents did not keep their hopes in secret. After having three sons, it just *had* to be a daughter.

But that was not to be. On April 4, 1853, the Lincoln home was again filled with the cries of a baby boy. For the first time one of their sons was named after Lincoln's side of the family—his father Thomas, who had died in 1851. The christened name did not last for long, however. The moment Lincoln saw his son being bathed, with his unusually large head atop a tiny wiggling body like a tadpole, the child was nicknamed "Taddie" or "Tad" for short. Although both the elder Lincolns had hoped for a girl, they spared no love for their new son.

Babies, generally, were special favorites of the Lincolns. When a neighbor, Mrs. Dallman, was too ill to nurse her own child (there were no formulas in those days), Mary offered her own breast milk. Each day Lincoln not only played with his own three boys, but dutifully carried the Dallman baby from around the corner to Mary's bedside. There, Mrs. Lincoln fed both children until Mrs. Dallman was well enough to feed her own baby again.

Lincoln's law practice prospered. While he was out riding the circuit, Mary used the funds coming in to raise the roof of the house at Eighth and Jackson. A team of carpenters knocked down old walls and braces and put in new, stretching the house from a story-and-a-half into two full stories. Walls boasted gold-trimmed mirrors over fresh wallpaper, while each chair or sofa added was a bit more elegant—and expensive. Often a servant came in to help with the cooking and cleaning. Special servants were hired when the Lincolns entertained, which was more and more often. There was no doubt that Mary Todd Lincoln knew how to spend money, and she loved to.

No expense was spared when Emilie Todd of Lexington came to visit the Lincolns of Springfield. If they could not have a daughter of their own, Mary saw no reason why her half-sister could not be treated like one. At eighteen, Emilie shared Mary's chestnut brown hair, her flawless white skin and her rosy cheeks. She also shared her taste for fine clothes.

Lincoln welcomed his houseguest, but his mind was on other matters. He frequently buried his nose in a book or a sheaf of papers, paying little attention to the world around him. More than once, one of the boys slipped away from his supervision and Abraham suffered Mary's scoldings. He was often late for meals and late coming to bed at night.

Perhaps his mind was on politics. His term in Congress had been only a taste; now he hoped for a full helping. He heard people share their feelings about slavery and read about it in the newspapers. The issue of slavery in the territories was tearing the country apart. No leadership came from the White House or out of Congress. As a lawyer in Springfield, Lincoln felt confined and helpless in such matters. But if he could become a United States Senator...

In this era Senators were not elected directly by the voters. Each state legislature had the responsibility of selecting the state's two senators. This procedure meant that only men with influence had a chance to win the office. Lincoln had spent years cultivating friendships among the men who served in the Illinois legislature, and by the fall of 1854 he was ready to make his move. It was time to select a new senator, and the gentleman from Eighth and Jackson tossed his tall black hat, full of legal papers, into the ring.

He worked hard to win the office, giving speeches wherever a small group assembled, writing letters, explaining his positions on the issues.

The selection was made on February 8, 1855. Fifty-one votes were required to win. On the first ballot, Lincoln led with forty-five votes. His hopes rose. Yet, as the balloting continued, support for Lincoln slipped. A man named Lyman Trumbull won the office.

Lincoln was bitterly disappointed, and his wife shared his disappointment. While, according to Emilie's journals, neither one displayed their feelings openly, Lincoln said years later that after his defeat in 1855 he intended to retire from politics and concentrate on his law career. He had a young, growing family to support. But his retirement from public life was to be short-lived. The controversy over slavery, that many believed had apparently been put to rest by the Compromise of 1850, was about to burst forth again—this time in flames hot enough to throw the country into its bloodiest war. Abraham Lincoln was not a man who could resist speaking out on the most important issue of his day.

Lincoln attempted to ignore politics. When he was summoned East on legal matters in the fall of 1857, he decided to take his wife along. The boys were left with relatives. The couple went to New York and Canada, where they stood in awe of Niagara Falls. It was the honeymoon they never had, and they enjoyed every minute. Back in

Springfield, they felt refreshed, and eager to resume their usual hectic pace.

Events were beginning to escalate. The Whig Party had been suffering from sectional conflict—disagreement between its northern and southern members over slavery—for decades. Finally, the pressure grew too great, and the party breathed its last breath and died. Clearly, a new political organization had to be born, one that would not splinter over the issue of slavery. Most of the members of the former Whig Party joined the new Republican Party.

The Republicans were organized around one chief issue—opposition to the extension of slavery into the territories. This issue of slavery in the new territories that were being brought into the United States had been brewing ever since American armies had won the Mexican War. Slaveholders, who lived primarily in the South, argued that the Constitution protected their right to own slaves, and the right extended to all parts of the United States. For a variety of reasons, many in the North disagreed. Abolitionists felt deeply slavery was an evil institution and had to be ended; many were willing to destroy the Union if that was the only way to destroy slavery.

Others in the North, including Abraham Lincoln, took a more moderate position. While he always made it clear that he personally felt slavery was evil, he also argued that the framers of the Constitution had recognized the institution of slavery, so there was no constitutional way to free the slaves in areas it existed in 1787. But he argued forcefully, and with increasing eloquence, that slavery should not extend into new territories.

Political leaders from the South, like Senator Jefferson Davis from Mississippi, were afraid that if slavery could not be extended the U.S. Congress would eventually be made up mostly of men from free states. What would stop these politicians from forcing through an amendment to the Constitution outlawing slavery? What would become of the South then, with its genteel landed aristocracy, and its gentlemen who considered it unseemly to bend their backs to physical labor? Increasingly, to men like Davis, it seemed that the only alternative was for the South to withdraw from the United States and form a separate nation.

The issue erupted into a white heat again in 1855, when Mary's old beau, Democratic Senator Stephan A. Douglas of Illinois, proposed the Kansas-Nebraska Act. This law

The Lincoln home, surrounded by political supporters, during the 1860 campaign. (Library of Congress)

would allow the people who lived in each territory to decide by a vote if they wanted to allow slavery to legally exist when the territory became a state. The members of Congress from the South embraced this idea; many members from the North felt betrayed by Douglas. Nevertheless, the law passed, and the slavery debate raged again. This time it would not stop until the nation's bloodiest war had decided the issue forever.

Lincoln was one of the men incensed by the Kansas-Nebraska Act, and he joined the Republican Party. As the division between the South and the North grew wider, as war clouds grew, Lincoln spoke out at every gathering he attended, attacking the new law and the South's contention that slavery be extended to the territories.

In the summer of 1858, Lincoln got another chance to grab a senator's slot, and this time the campaign would bring him national attention. Illinois Republicans tapped him to run against Senator Douglas. Douglas, a small man with a big voice, had earned the nickname "The Little Giant." Mary's feelings all rested in her husband's corner. "Mr. Douglas is a very little, little giant by the side of my tall Kentuckian," she declared.

People across Illinois got a good chance to size up both candidates before the election. The candidates debated in seven Illinois cities—Jonesboro, Charleston, Ottawa, Freeport, Galesburg, Quincy and Alton. Bands played, supporters carried torches and marched in nighttime parades. People munched barbecue sandwiches and sipped cool drinks as they listened to the two men argue the issues of the day. Over and over, Lincoln repeated his support for a strong United States. "I believe this government cannot endure, permanently half slave and half free." Mary followed the debates with interest, although she attended only the celebration held in Alton. Though it went against her nature to stay out of the fray, it simply would not have been proper to leave her children in order to go "politicking" with her husband.

Election day arrived on November 2. Heavy rains swept the state, keeping many voters away from the polls. However, when the ballots were counted, Douglas triumphed.

Despite his loss, Lincoln had left his mark. While the citizens of Illinois listened to his speeches, people across the country had read them in newspapers. And there were many Americans who agreed totally with Abraham Lincoln. He seemed a voice of reason in the midst of the increasingly shrill debate. Stephan A. Douglas went off to serve in the United States Senate, leaving the Lincolns behind in Springfield. But there was a rumbling in the nation—a rumbling that would shake the very foundations of the house at Eighth and Jackson.

"MARY, MARY, WE ARE ELECTED!"

By law, the Illinois legislature met every other year. Whenever the legislature met, the Lincoln home at Eighth and Jackson welcomed guests. When the Illinois legislature began meeting in February of 1859, the Lincolns were ready. Past political defeats had failed to dampen their spirits.

The man of the house was an able host. Abraham eagerly welcomed his friends and talked with each one. But he did not compare with his wife. Mary, always seeming to sport a new outfit, twirled and swirled from visitor to visitor. With the ladies, she chattered about children and the latest fashions. But she was just as able to talk politics with the gentlemen. It was clear to all that Mary often discussed the issues of the day with her husband.

It was equally clear that Abraham Lincoln entertained notions of running again for political office. The debates with Stephan Douglas had carried Lincoln's reputation far beyond Illinois boundaries. Invitations to speak flowed in from towns and cities across the country. He accepted as many as he could. Robert was off to Phillips Exeter Academy, a fine school in the East. At ages eight and six, Willie and Tad did not demand the constant attention of infants. However, Mary stayed home most of time. It was fine for a wife to be supportive of her husband, but most people did not want to see a woman campaigning.

There was nothing wrong with a woman simply traveling with her husband, though. During 1859, Mary kept her bags packed. The Todds seemed to be sprinkled in every nearby state, and she enjoyed family picnics and parties wherever she went.

But Mary was always glad to return to her sons. Not a day passed when she did not think about her beloved Willie. When Tad became ill and Mr. Lincoln was in Chicago, Mary sent a quick message. She wrote that "...our dear little Taddie is quite sick. The Dr. thinks it may prove a slight attack of lung fever..." She hoped that Lincoln might hurry home as soon as he could. He did just that, eager to be with his sick son and anxious to avoid Mary's wrath.

A newspaper illustration of the First Lady-elect with Willie and Tad, 1860. (Library of Congress)

Throughout 1859, Lincoln's image grew stronger. "The man is the voice of the North," one newspaper editor declared. "It should be listened to with respect and admiration."

Unfortunately, William Herndon was not achieving the same respect and admiration in Springfield. Lincoln's junior law partner was arrested for drunkenness, and was also accused of making false statements about prominent people. The reports angered Mary. Did the man not realize his actions could hinder her husband's future?

In February of 1860, Lincoln journeyed to New York to speak before the Cooper Union. It was important that Lincoln deliver a strong address about the nation. President James Buchanan's attempts to keep the country together were failing. He did not plan to run for re-election. If Lincoln could appear presidential, he might be the Republican candidate in May.

The Cooper Union was a workingman's group, laborers who repaired wooden barrels and casks. As Lincoln was introduced, the 1500 people present jumped to their feet and cheered. Then they sat down to listen.

"Some claim that our Constitution affirms the right of one man to own another as a slave," said Lincoln. "A true inspection of the Constitution will reveal no such right exists!" The audience applauded while Lincoln caught his breath and plunged on. "Wrong as we think slavery is, we can yet afford to let it alone where it is, because that much is due to the necessity arising from its actual presence in the nation; but can we, while our votes will prevent it, allow it to spread into the national Territories, and to overrun us here in these free states? If our sense of duty forbids this, then let us stand by our duty fearlessly and effectively. Let us have faith that right makes might, and in that faith let us to the end dare to do our duty as we understand it."

Did Mary hear the cheers back in Illinois that night? One might think so. The listeners stomped on the floor and yelped to the skies. Lincoln was a major voice of the Republican party—a clear and powerful voice. Who could better carry the Republican banner in the next election?

On May 18, 1860, the Republicans gathered in Chicago. Although according to the political style of the time, Lincoln could not be there, he met with his political friends in Springfield, leaving Mary at home to watch the children, wait, wonder, and hope.

At about noon the sounds of cannon echoed across Springfield. Telegraph wires carried the exciting news.

Abraham Lincoln had been nominated on the third ballot in Chicago. The lawyer donned his tall hat and excused himself from his friends. "There's a little woman down at our house would like to hear this," he offered. "I'll go down and tell her."

Mary more than shared her husband's pleasure; she surpassed it. So often when he had seemed uncertain he was doing the right thing, it had been Mary who urged him on. For years she had dreamed of this moment. Now it was here.

In the weeks and months that followed, the Lincolns stayed home in Springfield. In that era, Presidential candidates did not travel the country campaigning. They let their party supporters do that. Instead, Lincoln remained in the house at Eighth and Jackson. People constantly came and went, always being welcomed by the host and hostess of the house.

One night in August, over 6,000 people paraded by the Lincoln home. Torches lit up the night sky, bands played victory songs, and people cheered. Lincoln nodded and waved, hoping the people would not be disappointed in November. Mary stood beside her lanky husband, convinced that the election day crowd would be twice as large.

On November 6, 1860, the American people voted. The

Democratic Party had failed to agree on a candidate at its nominating convention in Charleston, South Carolina. The southern wing had nominated John Breckinridge, the northern wing nominated Stephan A. Douglas. Yet even another candidate, John Bell, was backed by the Constitution Union Party.

A large crowd gathered at the Springfield telegraph office on election night. Vote counts rolled in slowly. The hours crept by, and the news was sparse. Each state's results were met with either cheers or moans. Long into the night, everyone stood waiting for the results from the state of New York. Its vote would decide the election. Finally the telegraph operator announced the news—"Our Abe has won!"

The word spread quickly. The Republicans backing "The Railsplitter from Illinois" had stood firm behind their candidate, pulling in other voters too. He had captured 1,866,452 of the popular votes, compared to a combined total of 2,813,741 for his opponents. This time Lincoln did not have to make a concession speech, or bother with polite excuses. He slipped away from the crowd silently, wanting to be the first to tell his wife. Approaching his home, bystanders noticed his pace quicken and heard him exclaim in his high-pitched voice: "Mary, Mary! We are elected."

FIRST LADY

No President-elect, before or since, has faced the burden that Abraham Lincoln did when he left his beloved Springfield for the last time. In those days, a new President did not assume office until March 4 of the following year. From November of 1860 until March of 1861 the nation literally fell apart. Most Southerners saw Lincoln's election as the last straw, and felt they had no alternative but to form their own country. As the southern states began seceding, President Buchanan was frozen by indecision. Nothing was done to stop the states from renouncing all allegiance to the Union, or from seizing federal property, such as military installations, within their boundaries.

Public opinion in the North was divided. Some people wanted to let the South secede. Many abolitionists, for example, said good riddance to slavery, and to the people who supported a system they saw as evil; others in the North were not willing to fight over the issue. Lincoln knew that he would have to make it clear that his concern was the preservation of the Union, more than the ending of slavery, if he were to gain support for military action.

As tensions mounted, and Buchanan failed to respond, Lincoln began to realize that only war could bring the southern states back into the Union. For a man who had never shed blood in conflict, it was a painful decision. Mary Todd Lincoln, formerly of Kentucky, knew that if war broke out many of her relatives and friends would side with, and fight for, the South. Her proud family would be torn apart.

But Mary refused to let worries over future troubles interfere with her excitement. Mr. Lincoln was going to be the next President of the United States. She had been proved right those many years before when she had selected the gangly young lawyer over her other suitors. She was not shy about lording her good judgement over those who had tried to stop her from marrying her husband.

The train that chugged out of the Springfield depot that February of 1861 had a top speed of thirty miles an hour. The mechanical caterpillar inched its way northeast, stopping here and there to present Abraham Lincoln to the crowds who welcomed his arrival. For Mary, it was probably the most joyful time of her life. Once she even joined her husband on the back platform of the train when the smiling president-elect joked that it was time for people to see "the long and the short of it," and stretched his 6'4" frame above her 5'3" figure. The people loved it!

But not everyone was pleased that Abraham Lincoln had become the President. A plot to assassinate him was uncovered upon his arrival in Baltimore. Mary could not believe her ears! Who would want to do such a thing? And why? Yet Mary knew too well the pulse of the country. There were many from the South, her own beloved homeland, who would like to see Lincoln dead. "Resistance to Lincoln is obedience to God!" some declared. She knew too, that there were those who hated her as well. After all, what decent Kentucky lady would marry such a worthless, uncivilized scoundrel as Abraham Lincoln? No one seemed to remember that he, too, had been born in Kentucky. Many chose to regard him as some hayseed from the western wilderness. Yes, Mary knew what many people thought, and that awareness brought her headaches. For safety, guards smuggled Lincoln off the train in Baltimore and left Mary to enter the capital city with only her children the next day.

Mary dressed in a gown for the first Lincoln Inaugural, March 1861.
(Library of Congress)

On March 4, 1861, an anxious crowd flocked to the Capitol to watch the 16th President of the United States be inaugurated. Mary sat with government officials and listened to her husband attempt to patch up the sectional differences. Since the preceding December, southern states had begun pulling out of the Union. Whispers of war grew louder each passing day. Desperately, the new President wanted to pull the nation back together. "We must not be enemies," he said. "Though passion may have strained it must not break our bonds of affection. The mystic chords of memory, stretching from every battlefield and patriot grave to every living heart and hearthstone all over this broad land, will yet swell the chorus of the Union, when again touched, as surely they will be, by the better angels of our nature."

But the "angels" were nowhere to be found on April 12, 1861 when Southern guns fired on Fort Sumter, located in Charleston Harbor in South Carolina. By this time, Lincoln had accepted that only war would preserve the union, and he seized on the firing to call for volunteers to put down the rebellion and ordered a blockade of Southern ports. The nation was at war.

Certainly no one knew how the Civil War would end

when it first began. Most assumed it would be quick. A few weeks, perhaps. A month or two at the most. For whatever length of time it would last, it would be painful. Families would be divided, some young men choosing the Southern cause while their families, neighbors, and friends chose the Northern side. Mary soon learned there were those in her own family who considered her a "traitor."

Mary refused to be drawn into such conflicts. It was her job as First Lady to manage the social side of White House affairs. After all, her husband could not spend every waking hour running a war!

Lincoln's predecessor, James Buchanan, had been a bachelor. His niece had helped with his entertaining. But Mary meant for Washington society to know there was a new woman in the White House. She definitely wanted to make her mark.

Learning that the First Lady was entitled to her own dressmaker was happy news indeed! No longer would it be necessary to visit countless shops and stores looking for just the right fabric and style. Now Mary could order as many dresses as she wished, whenever she wished. She needed jewelry too—and new shoes would be necessary.

Thoughts of simply remaining in Washington to shop

disappeared quickly. New York City was so close. It would seem foolish not to take advantage of its many fashionable stores. . .

There were many parts of the White House that appeared dull and drab to Mary. As the war continued to drag on, she wanted nothing around her husband to be depressing. She ordered rich purple and gold drapes for one bedroom, green velvet carpet that cushioned every step for another. If more money was needed, Mary's answer was short and simple— ask Congress for it.

However, there were those in Washington who did not appreciate Mary's requests for more money. There were whispers about "that woman" in the White House who was busy buying satin and silk gowns while young soldiers lay soaked in blood on the battlefields of war.

Mary heard the whispers. She knew what many were saying. Yet if she did not entertain important guests, if she allowed the White House to be drab and dismal, would she not also be criticized? There was no way of pleasing everyone. The important thing was—what did the President think? One remark he made at a reception lifted her spirits.

"My wife is as handsome as when she was a girl, and I, a poor nobody then, fell in love with her." The President

The First Lady meets with a delegation of Native American leaders in the White House Rose Garden. (Library of Congress)

paused, gazing at Mary. "And what is more, I have never fallen out."

With Robert away at Harvard College, there were just Willie and Tad in the White House. Although both "Father" and "Mother" Lincoln loved both their sons, it was no secret that Willie was his mother's favorite, while Tad was his father's choice. As long as Mary had the love of Mr. Lincoln, and her son Willie, she could care less about the gossip. For the first few months as First Lady, despite the war that was going badly for the North, Mary was content in the bosom of her family. But her tranquility was to be soon shattered.

Less than a year after entering the White House, Willie suddenly became ill. The illness was probably typhoid fever, caused by the sewage that seeped into the city's water supply from the thousands of military encampments that had sprung up around Washington, D.C. After a period of high fever, Willie seemed to rally for his father's birthday on February 12. But his strength slipped away with the day.

Once again, father and mother took turns at their son's bedside. Surely memories of their beloved Eddie filtered back. But maybe this time it would be different.

It was not to be. Willie grew delirious with fever, and on February 20, 1862, William Wallace Lincoln died.

Lincoln grieved deeply, seeking solace in the hope that Willie was now at home with God. For Mary, the sadness was too much. She lay in bed for days, unable to rise even for her son's funeral. She cried out and wept, unable to eat or sleep.

Once more, Lincoln had to pull Mary out of her sadness. He knew his wife well. Pleading with her that her "three boys" could not live without her, he convinced her to live for them. Slowly, she gave in.

But life at the White House changed after the death of Willie. There were no more receptions and parties. Instead, Mary visited the hospitals in Washington. She visited the wounded soldiers, taking them cookies and tins of cake from the White House bakery and strawberries from the garden. Most of all, she talked and listened to stories of mothers, wives, and sweethearts. The hours slipped by and a nurse would remind Mary of the time. Off she would go, with promises to return. And she did.

When Robert Lincoln voiced his desire to join the war effort, Mary argued against it. "Is it not enough I have lost two of my boys?" But she could do nothing when both her son and husband agreed that it was a decision that Robert make on his own.

On January 1, 1863, Lincoln issued the Emancipation Proclamation. This document freed the slaves that lived in the South. This meant that when the war ended, and if the North was victorious, the South would no longer have a society economically based on slavery. But in the winter of 1863, the proclamation was only a document. The new Confederate States of America was winning most of the battles, and the end of the war looked to be a long way off. To shore up morale, Abraham decided to have a reception to celebrate his announcement, and, although Mary still did not feel like entertaining, she and her husband hosted a New Year's Day reception. How proud she was of what her husband had done. "It is a rich and precious legacy," she said, "for my sons and one for which, I am sure, and believe, they will always bless God and their father."

Not everyone in the nation blessed President Abraham Lincoln. The conflict dragged on and on. Bodies littered the battlefields; the South fought with determination. Northerners wondered why the man in the White House could not bring a quicker end to all the bloodshed.

The Retired Soldiers' Home outside Washington offered the Lincoln family a chance to escape the city heat and the sad memories of the White House. Often Lincoln and his

The gathering around the podium during Lincoln's presentation of the Gettysburg Address, November 19, 1863. (National Archives)

wife took carriage rides together, sharing private conversation away from the shadows of war.

One morning Mary rode back to the Soldier's Home from the White House. No sooner had the carriage started rolling when the entire vehicle began to shake. Before the driver could gain control, he was throw out and the horses ran away. Mary fell from her seat onto the ground cracking her head against a rock. Quickly she was taken to a hospital.

Mary's wound became infected. As doctors and family hovered nearby, she fell in and out of consciousness. For Lincoln, the trouble was doubly hard. Not only did his wife lay critically ill, but a terrible battle had been fought at Gettysburg, Pennsylvania. Reports of Union soldiers killed ran high, and although Confederate soldiers had been beaten, they escaped without capture or pursuit.

For several days, Mary lay near death. Finally, she regained her strength. But she remained in pain, and the doctors prescribed medications to ease the discomfort and the nervousness that left her sleepless. When she was first prescribed the drugs is unclear. She may have been given the sleeping medication chloral hydrate when Eddie died in 1850. Later in life, doctors gave her laudanum, an addictive narcotic. It was not uncommon for women of her

Abraham Lincoln shortly before his death in 1865. (Library of Congress)

time to be prescribed such drugs. Most doctors were mystified by women's health problems, and few understood the long-term impact the potions would have on the patient's mind and body. One fact is clear. The medicines contributed to Mary's emotional deterioration in her later years.

When she was well enough, the doctors advised her to travel. They were concerned about the strain of being in Washington during the war. They might well have been worried about her safety, too.

Everyone knew Mary Todd Lincoln was a Southerner. Some Northerners wondered if she might be a spy. Such gossip found many eager ears. Women, especially, were quick to believe the worst about the First Lady. Many of the ladies in Washington's social circles had been shunned or poorly treated at White House gatherings or city affairs. Mary kept a careful eye on her husband. A few words exchanged in private or a lingering handshake was enough to arouse her jealousy. "Father" Lincoln was hers, and she wanted there to be no question about that fact!

While those around her treated Mary with suspicion and bitterness, there were many in her birth family who could not understand her. Some called her "that traitor Yankee woman." Mary remained locked in her room whenever bad news arrived from Kentucky. Sadly, it came often. Her half-brother, Samuel Briggs Todd, died at Shiloh. Another half-brother, David, fell at Vicksburg; another, Alexander Todd, was killed at Baton Rouge; and Ben Hardin Helm, the husband of sister Emilie, at Chickamauga, Georgia. Names of former friends and neighbors dotted the casualty lists.

Each year of the long war seemed etched into Lincoln's lined face. He held day long meetings, and visited war camps. Mary returned to her buying sprees, visiting stores in New York as well as in Washington. She bought a new necklace, a fur, dresses, and shoes. Bills arrived daily, and by the summer of 1864, Mary became panicky. People were saying that President Lincoln would not be re-elected. Without a salary, there would be no money. What would happen? The people Mary told shook their heads. Why was there such need to buy so many things? Perhaps it was the head injury she received. But no, she had always been quick to spend money...

Mary's fears were erased in the November election. Lincoln easily defeated the Democrat, George McClellan. And there were rumors the Civil War was about to end.

By March of 1865, the rumors became reality. The Confederates were in retreat. Victory belonged to the North!

But there would be no revenge, not from the President of the United States. Mary, attired in a new inauguration dress, sat proudly behind her husband as he spoke on March 4, 1865. "With malice toward none; with charity for all; with firmness in the right, as God gives us to see the right, let us strive on to finish the work we are in...."

On April 9, 1865, the work was finished. General Robert E. Lee of the Southern Confederate states surrendered to General Ulysses S. Grant of the Union Army.

It seemed the entire world raced to the White House. The grounds were covered with bands and people singing "Yankee Doodle" and warm religious melodies. In a show of reconciliation, President Lincoln asked a band to play the Southern favorite "Dixie." No, there would be no hard feelings in this war. It was time to mend the wounds.

Mary was elated. Now it was time for joy in the White House. From the moment she had entered, there had been the sadness of a nation torn apart. War, those terrible four years of bloody war. Then there was Willie. Poor, poor Willie.

But those days were past. It was time for celebration. No more long faces, no more tears.

Friday, April 14, 1865 began with great promise. Robert

Abraham Lincoln's funeral procession down Pennsylvania Avenue, April 19, 1865. (Library of Congress)

returned from active duty in the Union Army. His return lifted his parents spirits as they went for their usual carriage ride that afternoon. They came back early, Lincoln feeling tired and Mary with a headache. They thought about giving up their plans to visit Ford's Theatre that evening. Yet people were expecting them to be there. A comedy was being performed, "An American Cousin," and Mr. Lincoln liked nothing more than a silly comedy to take his mind off his work. Yes, they decided, they had better go.

At about eight-thirty, the Presidential party arrived at Ford's Theatre. Major Henry Rathbone and Miss Clara Harris were their guests. The President waved to the audience who stood applauding, then settled down for an evening of pleasure. By the third act, Mary Lincoln sat close to her husband, her hand clasping his. "What will Miss Harris think of my hanging on to you so?" she whispered. The President gazed at his wife. "She won't think anything about it," he said softly.

Those were his last words. An actor turned assassin named John Wilkes Booth crept into the Presidential box. There was the sudden crack of a gun firing. Feeling her husband's body slip down, Mary tried to keep it upright. Then she became frantic, screamed, and fainted.

The Lincoln family home in Springfield draped in mourning. (Library of Congress)

President Lincoln, a bullet in his brain, was carried across the street to the nearest house. Mary was helped to his bedside where she kissed him, then fainted again. "Oh, my God," Mary sobbed throughout the night. At exactly 7:22 on the morning of April 15, 1865, Abraham Lincoln died.

Doctors and friends took Mary back to the White House. She would not go to their bedroom. A guest room was found, one Lincoln had never used. But she still could not sleep.

For five weeks, Mary Todd Lincoln remained in bed. She could not attend her husband's funeral. In unguarded parts of the White House downstairs, souvenir hunters carted off lamps and tables, snatches of drapery and carpeting. Finally, on May 22 of 1865, Mary said farewell to the White House. Robert and Tad came to take her away. She wanted to go back to Illinois, but not to Springfield. There were too many memories there. Robert could continue studying law in Chicago, and Tad could finish school too. As Mary unpacked, she learned the newspapers were still attacking her—this time for stealing those things the souvenir hunters had taken. Once more, Mary Todd Lincoln wept.

DOWNWARD PLUNGE

At his death, Abraham Lincoln left an estate worth over $80,000. It was to be divided equally between Mary, Robert and Tad. For the times, that should have been quite adequate for a widow of 45.

But Mary Todd Lincoln was not behaving in a normal way. She refused invitations from family and friends to visit. Yet she complained about being lonely. She feared the dark and insisted on being inside by nightfall. If people spoke in hushed tones as she passed, she was certain they were talking about her. And then there was always the issue of money. For years she had feared being in debt. It had never happened, yet she was sure it would. She felt the Republicans should help her. It was due to her husband that they had jobs. The idea was distasteful to everyone, yet Mary Lincoln felt it was fair. She grew more angry when she could not persuade anyone to help her.

For the first year after her husband's tragic death, Mary Lincoln seldom left her rooms in a Chicago boardinghouse. Widows were expected to mourn for that length of time. In the summer of 1866, Mary traveled to Springfield, where Lincoln had been laid to rest in Oak Ridge Cemetery. When his old law partner, William Herndon, asked to visit her, Mary accepted. He claimed he wanted to write a book about the late President Lincoln.

William Herndon had changed little. Mary remembered he liked to drink, and he smelled of liquor when they met in a hotel lobby. Out of respect for her late husband, Mary answered the man's questions. She was delighted to talk about "the most loving husband and father in the world."

Mary had scarcely returned to Chicago when she learned of William Herndon's activities. He was presenting talks about Abraham Lincoln that did not use the information Mary had given Lincoln's former partner. Herndon claimed that Lincoln had never loved Mary Todd, but his true love was a girl named Ann Rutledge, a girl who died when he lived in New Salem.

Mary Lincoln was devastated. Surely people would not believe such stories! Mary did not realize how many people she had mystified in the past. Her jealousy, her spending sprees, her strange headaches—there were so many tales. Some even wondered if she had played a part in her husband's assassination! Mary retreated to her boarding-house rooms.

Creditors came pounding on her door. From the time Lincoln had won election to a second term, Mary Lincoln had spent money without a care. Now she was no longer First Lady, she was just another customer. What to do? Mary decided to sell many of her finest gowns, furs and pieces of jewelry to pay the debts.

Using the name of Mrs. Clarke, Mary headed to New York in September of 1867. Surely her possessions would bring a better price on Broadway, but she did not want people to know who she really was. A President's widow selling her clothes publicly would surely be criticized, and she had had quite enough.

The truth soon came out. The brokers handling the sale wanted everyone to know that the items had belonged to Mrs. Abraham Lincoln. They persuaded her to write people she had known in the White House, and to tell them about the sale. She did, and the brokers published the letters.

People across the country were outraged. A president's

widow selling her clothes in public? It was claimed she wanted a fortune for one dress in particular—the one she had worn to Ford's Theatre the night of the assassination! It was said the dead President's bloodstains were still on it.

A humiliated Mary Lincoln fled back to Chicago, and locked herself in her room. "I suppose I would be mobbed if I ventured out," she wrote to a friend.

In October of 1868, Mary sailed for Europe. She hoped to find some peace in "a land of strangers." Fifteen-year-old Tad went along. Robert was now a practicing lawyer, and was recently married. In September, he had married Mary Harlan from Iowa. Mary was glad to have Tad to herself. Always cheerful and pleasant, Tad was growing so tall, like his father, and reflected many of his good qualities. The boy looked after Mary whenever she was ill, like her husband had. Yes, it was good to have Tad around.

Robert, however, was different. He always seemed ready to criticize, and wanted to give orders. In addition, his need for money was constant. After his marriage, his wife encouraged him to borrow as much money as possible from Mary to start his law practice and furnish their home. Robert needed little encouragement. If his mother was going to waste the money anyway, was it not better put to use helping

William Herndon, whose book *Life Of Lincoln,* contained many
unflattering comments about Mary. (Library of Congress)

him launch his career, and insuring that his wife live in the style she was accustomed to? The tension between Robert and Mary had already begun, and Mary was more than happy to leave her eldest son behind as she and Tad left for Europe.

Mother and son both fell in love with the city of Frankfurt, Germany. He enrolled in a school run by Dr. Hohagen, a respected teacher. The summer vacations would allow time for travel. Mary settled in for a restful time, away from peering eyes and ugly whispers. Her pen flew across stationery, letters flowing one after another to her family and friends back in America.

But the news from America grew more cheerful. Robert's wife Mary Harlan had a baby, Mary's first grandchild, and they had named the child Mary. On July 14, 1870, Congress voted a pension for Mrs. Lincoln of $3000 a year. Suddenly, life in their own country seemed more appealing; both Mary and Tad grew eager to return.

By the next spring, mother and son stood aboard the steamer *Russia*, heading for America. The ship rolled and tossed on the voyage, by the time it docked in New York, most passengers were ill. But Mary and Tad were in no mood to pamper themselves. They headed for Chicago on the first train.

By May, the Lincolns were together again. Mary thrived on her new granddaughter. Robert still seemed to seek out things to criticize her for, and his wife was not always friendly, the thought of future visits with the grandchild brightened the older woman's spirit.

The brightness soon dimmed. Tad caught a cold that would not disappear. One day, he would improve. The next, he would be coughing and running a fever. Soon it became obvious that Tad suffered from tuberculosis, a disease few people survived in the nineteenth century. Once again, Mary took her position at a son's bedside, wiping his burning forehead with a cool cloth, holding his hand and humming softly. She was well practiced at this form of nursing, too well practiced.

On July 15, 1871, Thomas Lincoln died. His mother knelt beside her eighteen-year-old son as he breathed his last.

Mary Todd Lincoln was exhausted and weakened by the six weeks of caring for her son. Now, he was gone. It seemed too terrible to believe. A husband murdered before her eyes, and three sons stolen away by death.

Seeking escape, Mary again traveled. Although she had

relatives across the country, not all of them wanted her in their homes. Many of the Todds still held bitter feelings about the Civil War. Just because the South had lost the conflict did not mean all had been forgotten. There were family members who believed the stories about her wild spending habits in the White House, that she bought grand gowns while boys died in battle. Herndon still gave his talks, insisting that Ann Rutledge was Abraham Lincoln's true love and that Mary Todd had meant nothing to him.

From one state to another Mary hopscotched, her son Robert scarcely able to keep up with his mother's moves. Friends wrote him of her strange behavior. She was afraid of the night, afraid of being attacked, afraid of being poisoned. Some of the behavior he saw for himself, such as her trip to Chicago where she expected to find Robert dead. When she found him well, she then refused to stay in his home. He had to take a room beside hers at a hotel in order to watch her. Then she wandered out, half-clothed, dazed and confused. "You're trying to murder me!" she screamed, when Robert pulled her back inside her room. She spent large sums of money, often carrying thousands of dollars on her person.

Robert decided something had to be done. How much

Tad with his father, February 9, 1864. Tad was the only family member ever photographed with Abraham Lincoln. (Library of Congress)

he was truly concerned for his mother's safety, and how much he worried that she would spend his inheritance before he could get his hands on it, is unknown. He always claimed later that he only wanted to protect his mother, but he did have his own lavish life-style to support. Ironically, like his father before him, Robert had married a woman who expected a high standard of living.

Whatever his motives, as a lawyer Robert Lincoln knew how he could gain control of his mother's affairs. It would not be pleasant, but it could be done. In the spring of 1875, Robert Todd Lincoln filed papers to have his mother declared legally insane.

SUNSET

"Legally insane."

After the one-sided testimony had been heard, the verdict was hardly surprising. Even Mary Lincoln appeared to take the news calmly. She showed no emotion when Robert leaned over her chair, his cheeks stained with tears, and tried to comfort her. She followed guards to her hotel room in preparation for the next day's ride to a nearby sanitarium.

For years Mary had longed for the day she could lie beside her husband in the Oak Ridge Cemetery. On the night of May 18, 1875, she attempted to hasten that end. Eluding her guards, she hurried down to the Chicago streets. From one local druggist to another she went, trying to purchase a deadly mixture of camphor and laudanum. One druggist, sensing her intent, appeared to fill her request. Yet he did not give her the laudanum which would make the mixture lethal.

By carriage Mary was transported to Bellevue Place, a small hospital thirty-five miles from Chicago. The head of the sanitarium, Dr. R. J. Patterson, escorted her to her room. It was spacious enough, boasting a large bed and dresser. But Mary knew she was a prisoner there, and that fact intensified her feelings against Robert.

Not that she would let him know how she felt. Better to pretend that all was well between them. That might shorten her confinement. She welcomed him warmly when he visited, and wrote cheerful letters. Other letters went out too, building and mending relationships of the past. Judge James Bradwell, and his wife Myra, who was the first woman to attempt to become a member of the legal profession in the United States, visited often, as did Mary's sister Lizzie and brother-in-law Ninian Edwards from Springfield. When the Edwards asked if they might care for Mary in their home, permission was granted. After all, she had been a model patient in the hospital.

Mary continued her good behavior in Springfield. No doubt the city contained sad memories, but Mary fought to stay in control of her emotions. Lewis Edwards, her grand-nephew, became a special friend. He seemed much like Tad. In nine months, another sanity trial was held. Ninian

Edwards swore in a statement that her friends all thought his sister-in-law "was a proper person to take charge of her own affairs." The jury agreed.

Three days after the trial, Mary Lincoln wrote Robert an angry letter. She had waited until she was judged "restored to reason," and during that time her anger at her son had grown to a white heat. She demanded the return of all her possessions that his wife had "appropriated." She continued, ".... You have tried your game of robbery long enough...You have injured yourself, not me, by your wicked conduct." The letter was signed simply, "Mrs. A. Lincoln."

That matter done, Mary made plans to return to Europe. There was too much in America that was cruel; she was tired of gossip and rumors. People could believe what they wanted. She no longer cared, and wanted only to be left alone.

Mary made a home in Pau, France. Mostly she kept to herself, spending her time writing letters, reading, or going for short trips around Europe.

Time was slipping by, and Mary's strength was going. In the fall of 1880, she wrote her sister Lizzie that she was coming back to America. "I cannot trust myself, any longer away from you—I am too ill and feeble in health."

Mary had no desire to see her son Robert. Yet when he came to Springfield in May of 1881 with his own daughter Mary, she agreed to meet with him. What grandmother can withhold her love for a grandchild?

In January of 1882, Congress voted to increase Mary Lincoln's pension $2000 a year with an additional gift of $15,000, one thousand dollars for each year since her husband's death. It was hardly affection toward Mary that brought the action. President James Garfield had been assassinated the previous September. Congress awarded his widow a pension of $5000 a year. It seemed only right to increase Mary's pension. She grumbled that the amount was "paltry" but she was not about to turn it down. With her vision weakening and problems with her back increasing, Mary needed every penny she could get.

There was little future left. Back in Springfield, the days found Mary Lincoln in her sickbed more often, having no desire to get up. Often she expressed a wish to join her husband and children who had "gone before."

On July 16, 1882, that wish was granted. Across the country, as people learned of the death of Mary Todd Lincoln, they reacted with a variety of feelings. There were

A later picture of Mary Todd Lincoln. After her husband's assasination, Mary continued to wear mourning dress for the rest of her life. (Library of Congress)

tears shed in some homes, while in other places people made cruel jokes about "that crazy woman of Lincoln's."

At the funeral, the minister spoke of two stately pine trees growing together on a ledge. Their branches and roots were interwined. Lightning struck down one, and the other appeared unhurt. But hurt it was, more than anyone knew. Everyone knew the minister was not talking about trees. But now Mary Todd Lincoln could be hurt no more.

EPILOGUE

Following the funeral services at First Presbyterian Church in Springfield, the body of Mary Todd Lincoln was transported to Oak Ridge Cemetery. She was placed in a vault beside her husband and three sons.

Robert Lincoln was never reconciled with his mother. Mary destroyed the will she had made before Robert had her declared insane, and often discussed leaving her money to charity. In the end she did nothing. Following her death Robert petitioned the court as the only surviving heir, and two years later was awarded $84,035.00—the entire Lincoln estate minus the cost of legal proceedings.

Robert lived on for half a century. With a law degree from Harvard, he pursued a highly successful legal and business career, and remained active in politics. In 1881, President James Garfield appointed him Secretary of War, a position he served in until 1886. After leaving Washington, he moved to a large and fashionable mansion on exclusive Lake Shore Drive in Chicago and resumed his business career. However, in 1889 he accepted an ambassadorial post as Minister to the Court of St. James in Great Britian, which he treated as a working holiday.

Tragedy occurred in his life when his son Abraham, nicknamed Jack, died suddenly of blood poisoning in Paris. Robert finished his ambassadorial duties with a heavy heart.

Back in the United States, he was offered the position of president of the Pullman Company, a fabulously profitable company that monopolized the manufacture and operation of railroad sleeping cars. He was an effective executive, and lived a sumptuous life, traveling in private railroad cars with a retinue of maids and butlers, and enjoyed the company of the most wealthy and influential people of his day. In fact, he grew so much a part of the moneyed elite of his era that he would grow angry when someone reminded him of his father's famous image as a railsplitter who was born in a one-room, dirt floor cabin. Strangely, considering the conflicts he had with Mary in later years, Robert much preferred to talk about the Todd side of the family. He felt much more allegiance to that "noble" heritage than he did the unknown,

Robert Lincoln attending the dedication ceremony at the opening of the Lincoln Memorial in Washington, D. C. on May 30, 1922. (Library of Congress)

illiterate dirt farmers from which his famous father had sprung.

Robert remained with Pullman until old age prompted his retirement in 1922. He lived the remainder of his life on his two estates, a winter home in the Georgetown section of Washington, D.C., and a summer home in Vermont, where he devoted himself to amateur astronomy. One of the few public appearances of his later years was the ceremony marking the opening of the Lincoln Memorial in 1922. Robert Lincoln died in his sleep in 1926, at the age of 82.

CHRONOLOGY

1818 Born December 13 in Lexington, Kentucky.

1839 Moved to Springfield, Illinois.

1842 Married Abraham Lincoln November 4, 1842 in Springfield, Illinois.

1843 Son Robert Todd Lincoln born August 1 in Springfield, Illinois.

1846 Son Edward Baker Lincoln born March 10 in Springfield, Illinois.

1850 Edward Baker Lincoln died February 1 in Springfield, Illinois.
Son William Wallace Lincoln born December 21 in Springfield, Illinois.

1853 Thomas (Tad) Lincoln born April 4 in Springfield, Illinois.

1862 William Wallace Lincoln died February 20 in Washington, D.C.

1865 Abraham Lincoln assassinated April 15 in Washington, D.C.

1871 Thomas (Tad) Lincoln died July 15 in Chicago, Illinois.

1875 Declared "insane" in Chicago, Illinois—confined to Bellevue Place in Batavia, Illinois, from May 20 until September 10.

1882 Mary Todd Lincoln died July 16 in Springfield, Illinois.

BIBLIOGRAPHY

Baker, Jean H. *Mary Todd Lincoln: A Biography.* W. W. Norton, New York, 1987.

Freedman, Russell. *Lincoln: A Photobiography.* Houghton-Mifflin, Boston, 1988.

Means, Marianne. *The Woman In The White House.* Random House, New York, 1963.

Nolan, Jeanette Covert. *Abraham Lincoln.* Julian Messner, Inc., New York, 1953.

Oates, Stephen B. *With Malice Toward None—The Life Of Abraham Lincoln.* Harper & Row, New York, 1977.

Randall, Ruth Painter. *Mary Lincoln—Biography Of A Marriage.* Little, Brown and Company, Boston, 1953.

Schreiner, Jr., Samuel A. *The Trials Of Mrs. Lincoln.* Donald I. Fine, New York, 1987.

Turner, Justin G. and Linda Levitt Turner. *Mary Todd Lincoln—Her Life And Letters.* Alfred A. Knopf, New York, 1972.

INDEX